America, My Country
Explorers

Christopher Columbus

By Moira Rose Donohue

Clarke C. Scott, M.A.
Content Consultant

Your State • Your Standards • Your Grade Level

Dear Educators, Librarians and Parents . . .

Thank you for choosing this *"America, My Country"* book! We have designed this series to support state Departments of Educations' Common Core Standards for curriculum studies AND leveled informational text. Each book in the series has been written at grade level as measured by the ATOS Readability Formula for Books (Accelerated Reader), the Lexile Framework for Reading, and the Fountas & Pinnell Benchmark Assessment System for Guided Reading. Images, captions, and other design and critical thinking elements provide supportive visual messaging and learning activities to enhance text comprehension. Glossary and Word Index sections introduce key new words and help young readers develop skills in locating and combining information. We wish you all success in using this *"America, My Country"* series to meet your student or child's learning needs.

Jill Ward, President

Publisher
State Standards Publishing, LLC
1788 Quail Hollow
Hamilton, GA 31811
USA
1.866.740.3056
www.statestandardspublishing.com

Cataloging-in-Publication Data
Donohue, Moira Rose.
  Christopher Columbus / Moira Rose Donohue.
    p. cm. -- (America, my country explorers)
  Includes index.
  ISBN 978-1-93881-304-7 (lib. bdg.)
  ISBN 978-1-93881-308-5 (pbk.)
  1. Columbus, Christopher--Juvenile literature. 2. Explorers--American--Biography-- Juvenile literature. 3. Explorers--Spain--Biography-- Juvenile literature. I. Title.
  970.01/5092--dc23
  [B]

2013934089

Copyright ©2013 by State Standards Publishing, LLC. All rights reserved. No part of this book may be reproduced, stored, or transmitted in any form or by any means without prior written permission from the publisher. Printed in the United States of America, North Mankato, Minnesota, April 2013, 121312.

About the Author
Moira Rose Donohue has a Bachelor of Arts degree in political science from Mississippi University for Women and a Juris Doctorate degree from Santa Clara University School of Law. She was a banking legislative lawyer for 20 years before she began writing for children. Moira is a published author of numerous poems, plays, and articles, as well as two picture books. She loves dogs and tap dancing, and lives in northern Virginia with her family.

About the Content Consultant
Clarke C. Scott holds degrees from Central Michigan University and has 33 years of experience as a classroom teacher, building principal and system-wide administrator. Clarke most recently served as Director of Middle School Education and Lead Director for History with Pittsylvania County Schools in Virginia. He enjoys hiking, kayaking, caving, and exploring Virginia's and our nation's history. He shares his adventures both above and underground with his wife, Joyce, and family.

1 2 3 4 5 – CG – 17 16 15 14 13

Table of Contents

At an Early Age 5

Portugal 7

Around the World 9

Call Back 11

Journey 1 – Land, Land! 13

Indians 15

Journey 2 – Popularity? 17

Journeys 3 and 4 – Chains 19

A Whole New World 21

Glossary 22

Sound It Out! 22

Word Index 23

Explore With Bagster 24

Hi, I'm Bagster!
Let's learn about Explorers.

Christopher went sailing at an early age.

Christopher Columbus was born in Italy in an area called Genoa.

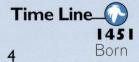

Time Line

1451
Born

At an Early Age

Christopher Columbus was born in Europe in the country of Italy in 1451. He lived in an area called Genoa on the Mediterranean Sea. Genoa was a busy shipping port for trade, or buying and selling. Merchants, a type of tradesman, made goods there and shipped them to sell in other places. Christopher's father was a merchant. He made and sold woolen cloth. He trained Christopher and his two brothers to join his business. But Christopher had other ideas. He wanted to sail.

No one is sure when Christopher first went sailing. Christopher himself wrote, "I went to sea at an early age." In 1476, he was sailing in the Atlantic Ocean on a merchant trading ship. His ship was attacked. Historians believe he floated to shore on a wooden oar. He landed in the country of Portugal, far from home.

Europeans wanted silk cloth and spices from Asia.

While Christopher lived in Portugal, he drew and sold maps.

Time Line

1451
Born

Portugal

For a sailor like Christopher, Portugal was a good place to land. It is on the west coast of Europe and close to Africa. In the late 1400s, Europeans wanted silk cloth and spices from Asia. These items were **scarce**, or hard to find, in Europe. But traveling to Asia by land was unsafe. Merchants wanted to find a faster, safer way to get there. Sailors tried to sail around the coast of Africa. Many left from Portugal. Portugal became the leader in sailing and **exploring**, or traveling to look for new discoveries.

In Portugal, Christopher drew and sold maps. He learned about **navigation**, or how to set a ship's course. Christopher used a type of navigation called **dead reckoning**. He set a course by measuring time and distance. He married Felipa Perestrello in 1479 and had a son, Diego. And then Christopher got an idea.

Around the World

In ancient times, people thought the world was flat. But educated people in Christopher's day knew the world was round. They thought they could sail west to reach Asia. But they didn't know how far away Asia was. And they didn't know that there was land between Europe and Asia. Christopher's idea was that Asia wasn't that far from Europe. He wrote to Toscanelli, a famous **geographer**. Toscanelli studied the earth. He told Christopher that the island of Japan in Asia was about 3,000 miles away.

In 1483 or 1484, Christopher asked King John II of Portugal for ships and money to sail west to Asia. But the king said that Christopher was wrong about the distance. The king said "No." He said Asia was too far away.

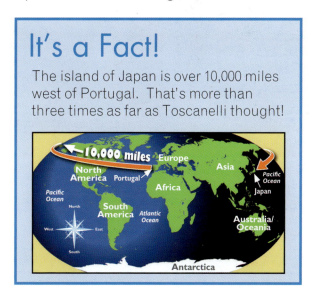

It's a Fact!
The island of Japan is over 10,000 miles west of Portugal. That's more than three times as far as Toscanelli thought!

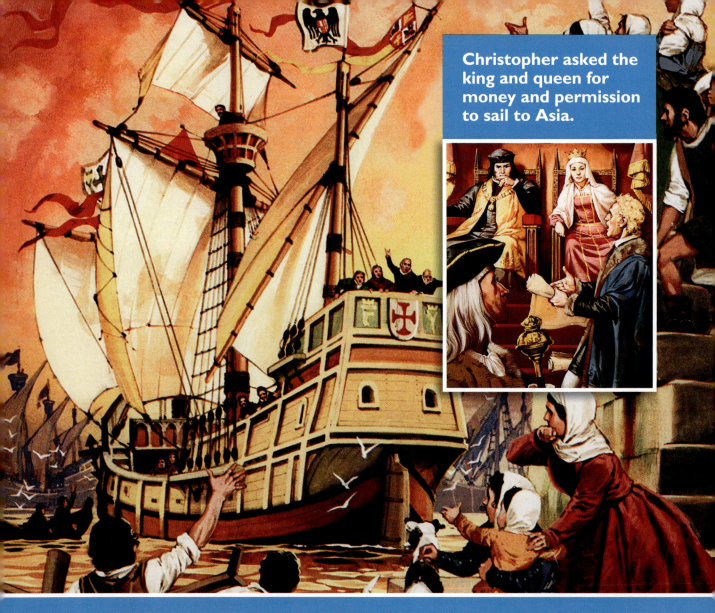

Christopher asked the king and queen for money and permission to sail to Asia.

King Ferdinand and Queen Isabella finally gave Christopher permission to sail.

Time Line

1451 Born

1485 Moves to Spain

Call Back

Christopher's wife died. In 1485, Christopher and his son, Diego, moved to Spain. Christopher hoped he would find the help he needed to sail. This time, Christopher asked King Ferdinand and Queen Isabella of Spain for money and permission to sail west to Asia. The king and queen liked Christopher. But they thought that it was too far to sail without maps and stopping for more food. Ferdinand and Isabella said "No," too!

Christopher made a good friend at the royal court. And he kept trying to get help from the king and queen. Then his friend told the king and queen that Christopher could bring them riches and find a sea route to Asia before other countries did. But in 1492, Ferdinand and Isabella refused again. Then they called Christopher back. They had changed their minds!

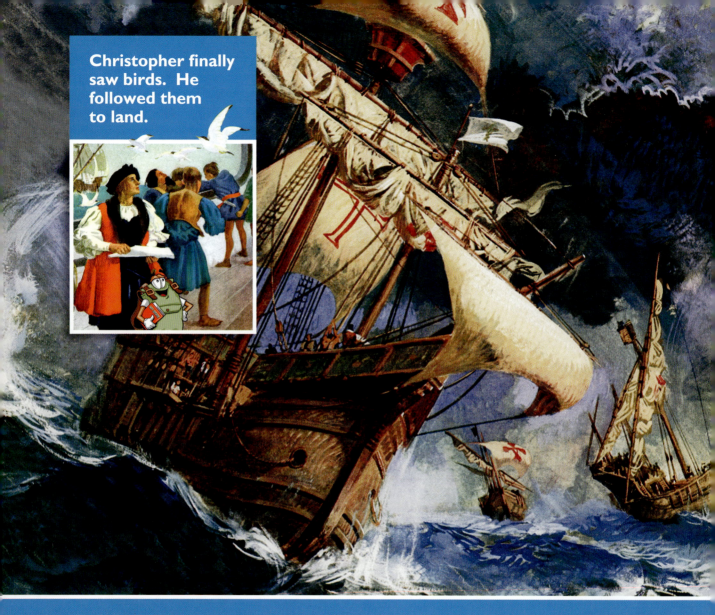

Christopher finally saw birds. He followed them to land.

Christopher set sail on the *Santa Maria*, the *Niña*, and the *Pinta*.

Time Line
- 1451 Born
- 1485 Moves to Spain
- 1492 Finds land

Journey 1 – Land, Land!

Christopher went to southern Spain to get his ships. He picked the *Santa Maria* as his supply ship. Then he found two small ships, the *Niña* and the *Pinta*. They were **caravels**. Caravels were small, fast ships invented by the Portuguese. They could sail ahead looking for land.

Christopher went to sea in August, 1492. He left from Palos, Spain. He kept a journal to record interesting facts about his journey. One day he wrote that he had seen flying fish with "two little wings like a bat." But Christopher also kept fake records about the distance he was traveling. The journey was taking longer than expected. The fake records kept the men calm about not finding land. In October, Christopher saw birds. He followed them. Early on October 12, 1492, a crewman yelled, "Tierra, tierra!" which means, "Land, land!" The birds had led Christopher to land.

It's a Fact!

Flying fish live in warm oceans. They push themselves out of the water with their tails and then glide in the air!

Christopher called the Taíno people "Indians."

Christopher claimed the island for Spain and called it San Salvador.

Time Line

1451 Born
1485 Moves to Spain
1492 Finds land

Indians

Christopher thought he had reached Asia, but he was mistaken. He had reached an island in the present-day Bahamas, in the Caribbean Sea. Christopher claimed the island for Spain and called it San Salvador.

The Taíno people lived on the island. Christopher thought he had landed on the East Indies islands in Asia. So he called the Taínos "Indians." The Taínos were gentle and friendly people. Christopher gave them gifts. Christopher explored other islands nearby. He claimed them for Spain, too. At Christmas time, the *Santa Maria* got stuck on the beach of an island called Hispaniola. Christopher left men there to start a colony. They built a fort with wood from the ship.

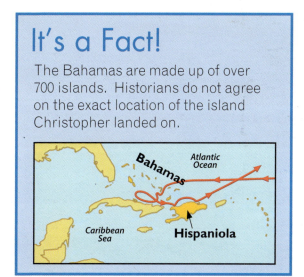

It's a Fact!

The Bahamas are made up of over 700 islands. Historians do not agree on the exact location of the island Christopher landed on.

Christopher had brought several Taíno people back with him.

Time Line

| 1451 | 1485 | 1492 | 1493 |
| Born | Moves to Spain | Finds land | Makes second journey |

Journey 2 – Popularity?

Christopher returned to Spain on the *Niña*. Ferdinand and Isabella welcomed him home with a royal party and wonderful gifts. Everyone believed Christopher had found a sea route to Asia. He was famous! Christopher showed the king and queen what he had found on his trip. He had brought gold and parrots. He had also brought several Taíno people back with him.

Ferdinand and Isabella wanted Christopher to go back to Hispaniola to explore. They also wanted to set up a colony. In 1493, they gave Christopher seventeen ships and livestock for the new colony. Christopher took more than 1,200 people with him, including his brothers. The colonists settled on Hispaniola. Christopher became their leader. But life was hard. The colonists got sick from illnesses on the islands. The Taínos got sick from illnesses brought by the colonists. And Christopher was not a kind leader.

Today, Hispaniola is made of the countries of Haiti and the Dominican Republic.

Christopher explored an area now called Central America.

- 3rd Journey
- 4th Journey

Christopher was put in chains and sent back to Spain.

Time Line

1451	1485	1492	1493	1498	1502
Born	Moves to Spain	Finds land	Makes second journey	Makes third journey	Makes final journey

Journeys 3 and 4 – Chains

The settlers told Ferdinand and Isabella about their problems with Christopher. So Christopher went back to Spain to talk to the king and queen. They still believed in Christopher. They still believed that he had found a sea route to Asia and would bring back riches. And they wanted him to explore south of Hispaniola. Christopher sailed again in 1498. This time, he sailed along the coast of present-day South America. Then he returned to Hispaniola. Christopher and his brothers were put in charge of the colony there. But they continued being mean to the colonists. And they made slaves out of the Indians.

Ferdinand and Isabella sent a trusted friend to check on the colony. He put Christopher in chains and sent him back to Spain. Ferdinand and Isabella forgave Christopher. They let him go free. In 1502, Christopher made his fourth and final trip west. He explored the area now called Central America. But he never found Asia. He returned to Spain.

It's a Fact! Europeans called the Americas the New World. Why might some people not call this the New World?

Christopher Columbus changed the world forever.

Time Line

1451	1485	1492	1493	1498	1502	1506
Born	Moves to Spain	Finds land	Makes second journey	Makes third journey	Makes final journey	Dies

A Whole New World

Christopher became ill. He died in Spain in 1506. He still thought he had found a way to sail to Asia but he couldn't prove it. Another Italian explorer, Amerigo Vespucci, realized that Christopher had not landed in Asia. He knew that Christopher had found someplace new. Vespucci called this place the **New World**. In 1507, a mapmaker and a teacher called it America.

Christopher was mistaken about reaching Asia. And he was not a good leader. But he changed the world forever. Christopher insisted he could sail west to reach land, and he did. He started the first permanent European settlement in the New World. And he set a course for European trade and settlement of the New World. In 1937, the U.S. government made a national holiday in honor of Christopher's discovery.

It's a Fact!

Many historians think that two Germans named Matthias Ringmann and Martin Waldseemüller first named the New World "America" on a map. They probably named it after Amerigo Vespucci.

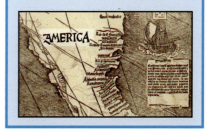

Glossary

caravel – A small, fast ship that could sail ahead looking for land.

dead reckoning – A way to navigate using time, distance, and direction instead of the position of the stars.

exploring – Traveling to look for new discoveries.

geographer – Someone who studies the natural features of the earth.

navigation – The science of setting the course, or direction, of a ship.

New World – The name Europeans called the Americas. The New World includes the continents of North America and South America.

scarce – Not plentiful. Something that is in short supply or is hard to find.

Sound It Out!

Amerigo Vespucci: **ah-mer-ih-go vez-poo-chee**
Caribbean: **care-ih-bee-uhn**
Diego: **dee-a-go**
Felipa Perestrello: **feh-lee-puh pear-ess-trel-lo**
Hispaniola: **his-span-yoh-luh**
Martin Waldseemüller: **vald-zee-mule-er**

Matthias Ringmann: **mah-thy-us ring-man**
Niña: **neen-yah**
Palos: **pah-lohs**
Pinta: **pin-tah**
Taíno: **tie-noh**
tierra: **tee-air-uh**
Toscanelli: **tah-skah-nell-ee**

Say these words like a pro!

Word Index

America, 19, 21
Asia, 7, 9, 11, 15, 17, 19, 21
Atlantic Ocean, 5
Bahamas, 15
believe, believed, 5, 17, 19
caravels, 13
Caribbean, 15
chains, 19
coast, 7, 19
colony, 15, 17, 19
countries, country, 5, 11, 15
dead reckoning, 7
Diego, 7, 11
discoveries, discovery, 7, 21
distance, 7, 9, 13
Europe, European, 5, 7, 9, 21
explore, exploring, 7, 15, 17, 19, 21
find, found, 7, 11, 13, 17, 19, 21
geographer, 9

gifts, 15, 17
gold, 17
Hispaniola, 15, 17, 19
ill, illnesses, 17, 21
Indians, 15, 19
island, 9, 15
Italian, Italy, 5, 21
journal, 13
journey, 13, 17, 19
king, 9, 11, 17, 19
land, landed, 5, 7, 9, 13, 15, 21
leader, 7, 17, 21
map, mapmaker, 7, 11, 21
merchant, 5, 7
money, 9, 11
navigation, 7
new, 7, 17, 21
New World, 21
Portugal, Portuguese, 5, 7, 9, 13

queen, 11, 17, 19
riches, 11, 19
sail, sailor, 5, 7, 9, 11, 13, 19, 21
scarce, 7
sea, 5, 11, 13, 17, 19
settle, settlement, 17, 19, 21
ship, 5, 7, 9, 13, 15, 17
Spain, 11, 13, 15, 17, 19, 21
Taíno, 15, 17
time, 7, 9, 11, 15, 19
Toscanelli, 9
trade, trading, 5, 21
traveling, 7, 13
trip, 17, 19
Vespucci, Amerigo, 21
west, 9, 11, 19, 21
world, 9, 21

Editorial Credits

Designer: Michael Sellner, Corporate Graphics, North Mankato, Minnesota
Consultant/Marketing Design: Alison Hagler, Basset and Becker Advertising, Columbus, Georgia

Image Credits — *All images © copyright contributor below unless otherwise specified. Maps: Edward Grajeda/iStockphoto unless otherwise specified.*

Cover – "The First Landing of Christopher Columbus in America" by Discoro Teofilo de la Puebla. **4/5** – Columbus: "Christopher Columbus on board his caravel," French School/Monastery of LaRabida, Spain/BridgemanArtLibrary; Boy: "When They Were Young: Christopher Columbus" by Peter Jackson/BridgemanArtLibrary. **6/7** – Map Maker: North Wind Picture Archives; Spice Market: Ivy Close Images/Alamy. **8/9** – Globe: BeBoy/Shutterstock; Toscanelli: Paolo dal Pozzo/Wikipedia; World: Alfonso de Tomas/Shutterstock. **10/11** – Sailing: "Columbus setting sail in the Santa Maria," by Angus McBride/Private Collection/Look & Learn/BridgemanArtLibrary; Monarchs: "Columbus presenting to Isabella & Ferdinand," by Angus McBride/Private Collection/Look & Learn/BridgemanArtLibrary. **12/13** – "Santa Maria," English School; Birds: Ivy Close Images/Alamy; Fish: FeatherCollector/Shutterstock. **14/15** – Columbus: "The First Landing of Christopher Columbus in America" by Discoro Teofilo de la Puebla; Ships: "Landing of Columbus in the New World," by William J. Aylward. **16/17** – Reception: North Wind Picture Archives. **18/19** – Chains: "Columbus in chains," American School/Private Collection/Look & Learn/BridgemanArtLibrary. **20/21** – New World: "Christopher Columbus and the discovery of America," by Cesare Dell'Acqua/De Agostini Picture Library/G. Dagli Orti/BridgemanArtLibrary; Map: Martin Waldseemüller/Wikipedia. **24** – Globe: Alfonso de Tomas/Shutterstock.

Explore With Bagster

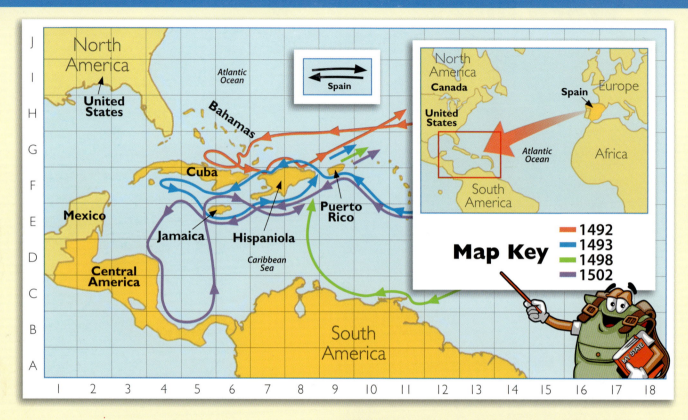

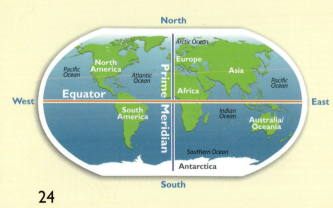

Words You Should Know!

continent – One of the great divisions of land on the earth. The seven continents are: Africa, Antarctica, Asia, Australia/Oceania, Europe, North America, and South America.

equator – An imaginary line around the center of the earth that divides the Northern Hemisphere from the Southern Hemisphere.

hemisphere – Half of a sphere (the globe) created by the equator or the prime meridian. The four hemispheres are: Northern, Southern, Western, and Eastern.

ocean – A vast body of salt water. The five oceans are: Arctic, Atlantic, Indian, Pacific, and Southern.

prime meridian – An imaginary line around the center of the earth that divides the Western Hemisphere from the Eastern Hemisphere.